Book One

Dedication

To my loving wife most of all. She taught me what love really means. To my family. Take care of your family and they will always be there. To my friends of the "Northern Conspiracy," a history club, for their support; both financial and with their presence. To the Rotary Club of Bedford - truly caring and honest people. And last but not least, my son Alex. Without Alex, the motivation would not have been there for me to overcome the stroke and get healthy.

Prologue

There is an old German proverb that roughly translates as: Don't carry your head too high, for the door is low. I carried my head high the year I turned forty. My life was full: happily married, thriving chiropractic practice, and a newborn son. Life was good. Then one bright, welcoming Tuesday in April of 1999, I discovered that the door indeed was low.

In a colleague's chiropractic office being treated for severe neck pain, we thought it was just the result of a strained muscle, too much stress and not enough sleep. It wasn't. After the treatment, the room began to move around me. Leaning up against a wall, hoping to stand I fell to the floor.

The staff helped me to a nearby couch. Lying there sweating, feeling helpless in disbelief; an ambulance was summed and my wife, Beth was called. Not only concerned and confused as to what happened to me but once in the emergency room, humiliation that I needed all this attention overwhelmed me.

Having recently earned a diplomate degree in chiropractic neurology, I understood that what I might be experiencing is a stroke. Gradually my world began to collapse in on me. Speech became increasingly difficult. My eyes would not focus. Nurses, doctors—even my wife—became blurry. Even taking a sip of water became impossible. Feeling lost, lying there on my left side all I could concentrate on was my right hand. This hand with the help of the left hand helped many people feel well, now it felt useless. I looked at it laying there, surrounded by the white sheets, hearing the hustle and bustle of the emergency room, the nurses calling for the doctor and the doctor giving the nurses instructions. Through it all my wife stroking my head telling me she loved me. The touch and her voice helped calm me. I thought of all the people I was letting down…my friends, my patients, my family and my new born son. What was going to happen to him if I die or not recover from this, what if it got worse? What was going to happen to Beth? At that point we had been married for 5 years. We'd know each other for 10. We were great for each other. I loved being married to her.

One of the doctors decided to do an MRI of my brain which revealed five infarcts in my cerebellum. This means that a localized area of my brain had received an insufficient supply of blood, most likely due to a blocked artery, which in turn had caused some of the cells to die. Since the cerebellum is the part of the brain that coordinates all of the body's movements, it explained why standing, swallowing and my vision were badly affected. It is funny how a simple thing like going to the bathroom can be a lasting memory of independence. It was the last thing I did before my whole world fell apart.

For me to have a stroke was almost impossible to

believe... it was a nightmare. Usually the elderly have strokes (1). People who don't exercise or eat right have strokes. Not fitting this profile a stroke for me was not right. It must have been a failure on my part, something was missed. I thought I had done everything right. I blamed myself.

Everyone has a birth date; well my new birth date was on April 15 in 1999. My new life began that day ; a life filled with miracles and hope, tragedy and loss. It is a life I never expected or planned to live and never thought that I would be healthier for the experience.

Chapter 1

My dreams and visions were of me being a wise healer that would come down from his home on a hill to dispense wisdom and knowledge about health and wellbeing. The solution for all the incurable diseases was a simple process that was over looked by the great researchers. The problem only needed someone with fresh eyes to figure it out.

After all this time and all I have been through I no longer think as I did when I was younger. Health and wellbeing is much more complicated than that and much more difficult to attain. The stroke had opened my eyes to the difficulty of attaining good health. It took 7 years to find my way to chiropractic again and I am still learning how difficult it is to remain healthy and stay in practice. Overcoming the physical limitations was relatively easy in comparison to the mental damage suffered. The damage is hard to fix let alone understand. You think you are fine, but you are angry, withdrawn, critical, depressed. These not only affect you but those around you. The cruelest aspect is that you don't realize it. Not wanting family members around, being upset when neighbors or family members drop in. Withdrawing from friends or just not wanting to hang out with people can be the results of many types of strokes. Before the stroke life was happy, fun and full of understanding. After the stroke it was filled with sadness, woefulness and suspicion. I am surprised Beth stayed with me. And not only that she had a big part in helping me become whole again. Looking at stroke and recovery as an opportunity helped me grow and understand my place and importance in my family, friends and patients. The stroke taught me that we all have a responsibility to ourselves and others to be the best we can be. Adversity makes us stronger and helps us see things that would not be revealed to us if life was without struggle.

I choose from a very early age to be a doctor. Not just a doctor, but a healer. That decision started a journey with many pitfalls and successes…leading through surgical assistant to a short order cook at a New Age restaurant. I thought I wanted to be a surgeon. Before applying to medical school I decided to work as a nurse's aide in an operating room at a local hospital. One day while waiting in the OR prep room I looked out a small window. There were birds flying in circles looking like they were both having fun and happy they were free to do so. Realizing from the moment I was not having fun I changed my path. I didn't want to be that kind of doctor. During this time I suffered from neck and back pain. A local Chiropractor helped me and even reduced my headaches. Impressed with his approach and how quickly I improved it was decided that was what I was going to do. A chiropractic career was for me.

My education at chiropractic school was as extensive as any medical schools the only difference being in medical school you learn about surgery and how to use drugs. The subjects, texts, testing, clinical expertise… etc. were the same. In fact we got many of our text books from the medical book store at Washington School of Medicine in St. Louis.

Human anatomy is the foundation of understanding normal human physiology. As a consequence it was one of the first classes given. Each team of five students was assigned a cadaver for the first two semesters. That is a whole year of dissecting and studying the same cadaver. In other words this was our body to have and to hold, to learn from and inspect for a year. It was one of the most fascinating years of my life. Before this I never fully understood the way the physical aspects of our body and how they are connected to make it all work. Actually seeing and touching the muscles that help us walk, sit, swim, bike was in a word breathtaking. Following the course of the blood vessels and nerves and realizing where they connect helped us understand how integrated everything is. It is almost as if we were given a key to the secret of life. We were both humbled and empowered by this.

One of the draw backs of the anatomy lab was the smell of the chemical formaldehyde, which was strong and distinct. It has been described as the most unholy smell that exists today, even worse than rotten eggs. So you can imagine what the cadaver lab smelled like and can also imagine what it was like to spend a couple of hours a day studying there. The formaldehyde was necessary to prevent the cadaver from rotting. That being the reality it was necessary to occasionally treat the cadaver with formaldehyde, or it would rot. This was done by covering the cadaver with cloth and pouring the formaldehyde on it so that it would soak. This was usually done once a week after we finished studying for the weekend.

Not only did it preserve the cadaver, but the smell permeated everything. Lockers were provided to keep our lab coats and other clothing articles. The smell of course got into the clothes so much you didn't want to bring them home or your home would smell like formaldehyde. At the end of the year of study the contents of the locker were put in the trash. No amount of washing would get rid of the smell.

It was difficult reconciling that this cadaver was once living and breathing. We couldn't help discussing what her life was before she died. We gave her a name (Mary), a husband (Bob) and children (3). It made it bearable. We were grateful to her for donating her body so we could study. The knowledge attained stayed with me even to this day. It was an invaluable experience. No pictures can fully help you comprehend the complexity and beauty of the inside of our bodies. No longer was I complacent about learning. I was driven to learn as much as I could.

Our first year wasn't just learning about anatomy, but how to apply what we learned. What makes chiropractic education different from medical education is medicine looks to treat with drugs and surgery, chiropractic treats with manipulation, exercise and nutrition. Manipulation or adjusting is the treatment of choice of most chiropractors and sets us apart from other health care providers. Manipulation is a method that was developed in 1895 to treat what is called the "Subluxation Complex."(1) Or better "Segmental Dysfunction." This dysfunction is usually located in the spine. The spine is made up of 24 moveable segments. These segments relate to one another by way of motion and they move by way of joints. These joints are made up of the same tissues that make up a knee or finger. If the normal motions of these joints are altered, pain and discomfort can result as well as other nefarious issues. There are a large amount of sensors located in the joints of these segments. These sensors communicate with the brain, muscles, and blood vessels other nerves and other pain nerves. So the theory is, if there is a segmental dysfunction there can be not only pain but consequences for the brain, blood vessel, and nerve function. The theory further stipulates that by manipulating these segments appropriately you can reduce pain, increase proper blood flow, help nerve communication and positively influence brain function. The core skill and art of chiropractic was to find this subluxation complex or segmental dysfunction and treat it with manipulation.'

One of the nagging questions I had back then was why do we get this subluxation complex in the first place? That I learned many years later and is one of the amazing consequences that came about because of my stroke. Try to remember that nagging question as you read this book, because I believe there might be an answer.

Chapter 2

I started practice in Massachusetts in 1986. Twenty years almost to the day after it was legal to do so. My brother said it was a nice place to live. So yep, it was Boston, Massachusetts. It is funny how we choose, or how if we don't choose, life chooses for us. My first few years of practice were filled with many triumphs and many failures. Times were both hopeful and difficult. There were many moments there was no way of knowing were my next dollar or meal was going to come from. Massachusetts, I found out later, just made it legal to practice chiropractic in the late 1960's, so there were many war stories about the early days from the old guard chiropractors. These stories reminded me of the days of prohibition and speak easies. Many Chiropractors practiced out of their homes or in non-descript buildings or alley ways. Payment was always in cash and the price was whatever the patient thought was appropriate. Many chiropractors were jailed for "practicing medicine without a license." Since it was legal to practice in New Hampshire, the border between New Hampshire and Massachusetts had many chiropractic offices. Once in practice for a while, patients told me stories about how they had to go across the border for a treatment. That time produced many legendary chiropractors. Individuals would travel 60 to 70 or more miles to see a chiropractor in NH. Finally the pressure to allow Chiropractors to practice in Massachusetts got too great to ignore. One brave chiropractor stood up and pushed hard to get the governor to sign into law legalizing Chiropractic. That was on June 28th 1966. (1) At that time there were only 38 chiropractors in Massachusetts. My license is number 1085.

Starting as a junior doctor for a chiropractor who practiced in Somerville was one of those decisions looking back on you wonder why you made. That was one of the failures. The chiropractor I worked for had been in practice for over 15 years. The chiropractic's office manager was her live-in partner and their relationship was dysfunctional at best. There were times when I would get to the office in the middle of a yelling match. Luckily it was a big office so they could go to one end of the practice so the patients could only hear a small roar. This made it difficult for me. I was at times placed in the middle of their arguments. I was young and wanted to learn as much as I could about running a practice. The ins and out of the law, how to advertise and let people know you are there, how to process patients and what to charge, what hours to operate and how long to treat patients. This was not the place I was going to learn all this.

The situation got so unbearable and I wasn't learning what I needed, I decided to give my notice and become what in the industry is called a vacation relief chiropractor. This was one of the triumphs. Most chiropractic offices were served by a single practitioner so if the doctor wanted to go on vacation he or she had two options. Close the office or hire someone to fill in. I became a 'fill-in' for the next year-and-a-half. This was anything but easy. You see, patients become really attached to their chiropractor. They are not interested in seeing anyone else. It's easy to feel inadequate when someone states. "You are not like Doctor Smith" or "Doctor Smith would do that differently." Needless to say I didn't see a career in relief practice. But the experience was invaluable. I got to improve my chiropractic skills. I saw many different kinds of illnesses and learned different ways of treating them. Also I got to experience multiple ways of running a chiropractic office…some successful ways and some not so.

Ending up in Concord Massachusetts as an associate doctor was a dream come true for me. History was all around me. History was one of my passions and especially revolutionary war history. The British were driven back over the Old North Bridge which was a five minute drive from the office. There are homes that have bullet holes still in them. Meriam's Corner was just down the street from the office, this is where the Colonial Militia ambushed the British who were trying to get back to Cambridge. The next town over was Lexington, which was the town where the first shot of the war was fired. Alcott, Thoreau, Emerson and more lived, worked and walked the streets of Concord. Their homes were preserved and made into museums. Concord was perfectly situated to see all the legendary beginnings and sites of the country. Plymouth Rock, Plymouth Plantation, Bunker Hill, Boston Tea party, and many sites related to King

Philip's War, where the Native American Indians nearly drove the colonists back into the sea. All this was a bonus. There were never a lack of things to do on my days off.

Being young and naive there was a lot to learn about running a practice. We treated neck and back pain. Looking back, honestly easy conditions to treat, nothing exciting or challenging. We advised every patient that they needed a set number of treatments over the course of six to eight months to completely fix their problem. Everyone was treated the same. Insurance was covering chiropractic so it was easy to sell the multi-week approach. However, there were many instances where the patient was much better in just a few visits. Instructed to keep continuing treatment, I soon became disillusioned. If a patient had no pain and full range of movement, why continue to treat them? Wouldn't it be better to say you're better, come back if you need to? At that time the impact of life style, food and exercise was not even considered.

My questioning did not go over well. *Pain is not a good indicator of health*, I was told. *Problems could be lurking that need to be treated so they don't become big problems.* I have come to learn that is a true statement. The difficult part is how you deal with this.

That was the first time I asked why patients have problems in the first place. Maybe we could treat the underlying problem, not just the pain. Patients could get back to living. Isn't that what we all wanted?

Chiropractic Neurology (2) seemed to hold a possible answer. After my first class it seemed that the gates of knowledge and heaven opened and poured its knowledge about health on me. Could this be what was missing?

Chiropractic Neurology taught me the *"why"* of pain, posture, muscle weakness, and chronic pain. *Why* is the body the way it is. *Why* it works the way it works and what makes us unique. It was all there for me to learn. Being able to understand and apply my knowledge to help someone who had suffered with pain for years and do it quickly and have a solution for them without needing to be treated once a week for the rest of their life was looking like it was possible. I delved right in and soon spoke with my boss about my desire to change the way we practiced. He wanted nothing to do with it. Stating that "I will start my own practice," he answered "You have a week." I was out of a job that quickly. Not something planned for, but luckily finding an office space was easy and my office was up and running within a week. I will be forever grateful for the landlord who gave me three free months' rent, and just believed in me. And the equipment supplier who floated my equipment costs for six months, most of all Beth, who stood by me and encouraged me to believe in myself. When doubt filled me, she showed none. My mother, sister, brothers and father were all positive about the move. They all believed in my skills and knew my practice was going to be successful and that it was the correct move for me. Being blessed and finally on my own filled me with joy, enthusiasm and hope for the future.

Studying and taking courses in Chiropractic neurology while running a full time practice was challenging but rewarding. Too fully take advantage of the program it was necessary to enter into the Chiropractic Diplomate program. The challenging part was not only the complexity of the material to study, but the time commitment. It was and currently is a three-year program requiring extensive course work, practice application, multiple exams, and a final two-day exam and a thesis paper which needed to be defended. Not only this, but falling in love and being involved in a local charity organization called Rotary filled my days to the point where there was very little free time. I actually became president of that organization. We raised money for everything from a new ambulance for the local EMS to Scholarships for local college bound students to literacy projects in third world countries. Never a dull moment made life full and rich and today my life is even fuller. I received my diplomate in 1991, but the learning did not stop there. New research and new ideas needed to be studied and learned constantly. My practice continually changed with the understanding of these ideas and research findings. Mistakes were made, but there were many successes and my reputation grew.

    This all lead to the development of a rehabilitation center focused on improving muscular function and concentrating on core strength to help with chronic back pain. There were tools used to determine the specific therapies needed to help correct a patient's chronic pain, migraines, vertigo…etc. From machines that analyzed how well patient's back muscles contracted to simple images that help a patient's eye movements affect the brain in order to help their back muscles function better. Blind Spot Mapping (3), which was just starting to be developed, was a simple method to determine any brain weakness. Blind spot mapping can help with a new chiropractic tool called unilateral Manipulation (4); unilateral manipulation can play a big role in brain rehabilitation. It is the process of selectively activating certain parts of the brain to strengthen function, thereby restoring balance to the brain. These were just a few of the exciting developments of the early nineties and the future was laden with possibilities for discovering more about how the brain works. It dramatically changed the way patients were treated. No longer was there a cookie cutter approach putting all patients on the same program no matter what their problem. Every patient was treated uniquely, thus their specific problem was addressed and thus they improved rapidly. It was gratifying to finally have patients improve to the point where they were released from care with the correct tools in order to keep themselves healthy.

In 1993 my soul mate and I were married. We moved into our new home, with great neighbors, wonderful family and friends. Life was turning out to be good and satisfying. The next six years had its ups and downs, but life was assured. There were honestly no major adversities to worry about. Looking back on those six years any issues were self-imposed.

Generally our brains are hard wired for adversity. The brain gives more attention to negative experiences over positive ones because negative events pose a chance of DANGER. By default, the brain alerts itself to potential threats in the environment, and... THEN awareness of positive aspects suddenly takes a lot more deliberate effort." (We become hyper-focused on the negative, so we have a hard time seeing, hearing, or feeling positive.)

    I never imagined that my health would be one of the biggest negatives

Chapter 3

A lump of flesh, no ability to move, no sense of smell no sensations or sense of what was happening. It was as if my brain forgot how to process the world. Life seemed unreal like it was a dream or what happened really did not happen. My body had no self-control. The faces of my doctors and nurses were dark and blurry. The doctors talked to the nurses in phrases that were hard to comprehend. Most everything was hard and seemed like it was getting harder. My life felt like it was slipping away; it seemed the only option was to give up. Death seemed close.

In addition to all that, there was knife-stabbing, skin-ripping pain. The right side of my face felt like a wild vicious animal was clawing at my eye and cheek. In addition, my right eyeball had a sensation that a needle was being driven into it. And there was more. My left arm, hand and leg felt like someone poured gasoline on them and set them ablaze and at the same time they felt like they were frozen. It was truly unbearable until the morphine kicked in. The morphine took away the pain and the blackness that was enveloping me. It eased the hopelessness. It made the whole experience seem more like a dream.

My family came from New Jersey to visit me that first week. My nephew went to school in Boston and was a near constant presence. My wife was a pillar of strength, caring for our newborn while her husband was in a hospital bed unable to move or speak above a whisper. Later, she'd tell me that my eyes were rotating violently. Not unlike a crazy, googley-eyed cartoon character. That explained the inability to see the faces of my loved ones, doctors and nurses. She held my hand; sometimes for hours. Her calming presence allowed me to be calm. Maybe she's the reason I never panicked. Maybe hopeless at first, but I did not panic. Eventually because of her the hopelessness faded to a desire to overcome. My wife took my stroke in stride, which allowed me to do the same. I owe her a great deal for that.

It was not possible for me to remember the many visitors. It was a tremendous outpouring of love and support. This helped me survive those first few weeks. This helped me learn my first lesson:

If you truly care about and love others they will care about and love you. We are all there to help one another through the good and bad times. We are not alone even when we think we are. All we have to do is ask.

Within a few days, we celebrated my blood pressure stabilizing. Since the stroke it was on a roller coaster ride: sometimes too high and sometimes too low. Unfortunately my symptoms got worse. I was dizzy all the time. I couldn't open my eyes. When I did, my world spun out of focus making me nauseous. This just made everything else more difficult to deal with. I just didn't know if things were going to get better. When I could ask and understand the doctors had no answer for this. Was it ever going to end? Would this be the way life will be? It just seemed like a mystery. Why were my eyes like this? I fought hard not to be hopeless. I had to be strong for Beth and my son. She wasn't about to give up on me so there was no option for me but to keep working.

Being transferred to another hospital's intensive care unit to be closer to my wife's work, the head neurologist and his team of neurology students took over my care. They tested my reflexes; poked prodded so many times it became a blur. But they made me feel special. After all, it wasn't every day that they got to examine a forty-year-old stroke survivor. I was somewhat of a celebrity.

After a few days Beth worked her magic and got me transferred to a private room. Luckily Beth was able to extend her maternity leave so she was able to visit me often. She knew the nurses and made sure they took extra good care of me. There was a great deal of alone time in a morphine-induced painlessness. The morphine gave me vivid hallucinations and disturbing dreams. Behind prison bars that were on fire entombed me, holding me back and it created a hell that could not been escaped from. Feeling trapped and hopeless now it was evident that I had a view of my subconscious without knowing it.

My ultimate diagnosis was a dissection of the vertebral artery on the right side of my neck that sent tiny little plaques into my brain's circulatory system. (1) The dissection, or tear, causes blood to enter the wall of the artery and form a blood clot. The artery wall thickens and impedes the flow of blood to the brain. This basically shut off areas of my cerebellum which regulate those parts of my body that now could no longer be controlled. This was the long explanation for why walking, speaking, and vision were so difficult as well as the ever present excruciating pain.

Nociception (2) is the scientific name for the sensations that come from your body. You do not perceive a sensation as pain until it reaches your brain where it is processed by the cerebellum. Putting your hand on a hot burner is a necessary pain you want your brain to feel so that you will pull your hand away to avoid burning it. You don't want to feel pain from the feeling of a sock or shoe or pant leg against your skin and you don't unless the part of the brain that deals with this is broken. Then every touch, even if there is no discernible pressure, can be painful. The area of my brain that regulates *nociception* was affected by the stroke and so I had tremendous pain and numbness. The right side of my face felt asleep, missing. My right fingers numb to everything. My left side was no better. I was numb from my neck down. At times this was overwhelming. It was all too much to deal with all together. There were so many problems. The only way to deal with them was ignore those that were not immediately important. My walking, and balance as well as my eyes were priority to me. Feeling that if they didn't get better, nothing else was going to get better. Soon my goals were clear: First walk, then balance and then eyes. The rest will have to wait till those are better.

These scattered symptoms are not surprising if you understand how the brain works. When you have a brain injury such as a stroke, concussion, or some type of metabolic neurologic disorder, the brain goes through a process called *diaschisis.*(3) Damage to one area of the brain causes other areas to function incorrectly. The parietal lobe is the part of the brain which deals with pain perception after it is processed by the cerebellum. It communicates directly with the cerebellum. The right parietal lobe has a map or impression of the left and right sides of the body. The left lobe has a map of the right side of the body only so if you have symptoms such as numbness, pain and burning on both sides of the body, chances are your right parietal lobe is affected.

An added complication is that your brain becomes inflamed after a stroke. Its own immune system kicks in and starts cleaning up damaged nerve cells. This is all well and good, but the brain's immune system is too efficient. The cells that do the cleaning up are called *Microglia* (4) cells. In their assault on dead or damaged cells they are like Chihuahuas with Uzis on crack cocaine. They are fervid and clumsy. As they clean up the damaged cells, they damage other cells and eliminate them. If the process is not stopped, they can do a lot of damage before they are finished. This is why the condition of the brain tends to worsen over time. It is also interesting in that concussions work the same way. A concussion can cause these microglial cells to get out of hand as well.

During my stay in the hospital, doctors and nurses continued to try to stabilize me. Eventually able to walk, albeit great deal of help wasn't easy but I walked! Walking so soon after the stroke was very encouraging, but Beth was a bit reserved. She had doubts, but God bless her she didn't let me know her concerns:

I watched him walk with a walker and people on either side of him. I thought, oh – this is good to see, but I couldn't quite imagine what his status would be in a week, a month or year. Not only was he having such tremendous trouble walking, but his vision was so problematic.

Two weeks after my stroke, in May of 1999, an ambulance transported me to New England rehabilitation hospital which aims to bring stroke and other brain injury victims back to some semblance of their prior lives. Regaining what was lost would be necessary if there was any chance of returning to the life I once knew.

Chapter 4

The only thing I remembered from the ambulance ride to the rehabilitation center was the white ceiling of the ambulance and being well taken care of, it wasn't possible to focus on anything else. When they wheeled me out of the ambulance the air was cold and crisp. A nurse said, "I'm here to take care of you". She seemed young, she was blond and she might have been pretty. My eyes would not let me make anything else out. Being transported in a wheel chair to a stretcher to a bed and my new home, she made me feel special, tucking me in like a newborn. She was and is a great nurse. My wife was there to ensure I wasn't alone. She was supportive and hopeful. Like always, she made my survival possible.

The hospital wing was very noisy. There were a lot of sick people in the brain injury ward and patients with brain injuries can be loud. (1) Often, a brain injury causes a loss of inhibition, so survivors can be raucous and inappropriate. There was one individual whom I never saw, but heard screamed and yelled "Help, Goddamit, help me," and plenty of other expletives.

All my symptoms were unchanged when admitted to the rehabilitation hospital: unable to walk or sit up in bed without assistance, could not transfer into a wheelchair without help, my eyes would not focus, and still could not speak above a whisper: Couldn't shake the pain: Worse still, it was impossible to shave, take a shower or wash my hair. This part drove me crazy because my appearance meant a great deal to me. That was my mother's fault: Being clean shaven, hair in the right place (no bed head), finger nails clipped and clean, and hands smooth along with a clean body was just normal for me. A shower a day was a minimum. This was just not possible though. Not being able to see myself clearly in the mirror let alone shave or clip my finger nails made it impossible to keep to that normalcy. My hair just got longer, matted and itched like crazy. Not having the ability to make myself clean and feel clean was just another loss of my humanness. In addition to this when water touched my left side it was painful. It felt like shards of glass ripping my skin. Later after being finally home there were times my son would put his hand on my leg and it took all my might not to scream out in pain. It felt like his fingers were razor blades. It was a challenge to slowly move his hand from my leg without letting him know how much it hurt and luckily he was not old enough to understand. Being as normal as possible with touch took a great deal of will power and energy. My family didn't know how much pain it was to hold hands or to simply touch my leg. Luckily this did improve over time. That painful experience is no longer an issue. Oddly this was a clue to getting better I was not aware of. Even if the brain was damaged it needed stimulation to get better. (2) Even though the stimulation was painful in small doses it actually helped my brain heal.

The restrictions on eating were another irritant. Because my right vocal cord was paralyzed, eating solid food was out of the question, so it was thickened water. This was what was called thickened nectar. (3) Approximately as thick as a milkshake. Common "natural" nectar thick liquids include, tomato juice, and buttermilk. Nutrients were added to the water like vitamins, minerals and protein. It did not taste nearly as good as tomato juice. As a matter of fact it tasted like unflavored jello only a lot slimier and nasty. It was more the texture that was nasty. Luckily I couldn't taste it since another aspect of my stroke was the loss of smell and taste. Yes the list of lost abilities goes on and on. As unappetizing as it was, it was the key to my survival. If my food was not carefully ingested it could easily flow into my lungs and infect them with pneumonia, a particular danger to recovering stroke victims. It would take the recovering of my speech and the use of my one good vocal cord in order to reduce the risk of aspirating my speech. There was a lot of work to do.

  My old life was over. Simply standing and walking to the corner coffee shop, talking to my neighbors or just going to the bathroom without help was out of the question. In other words, someone would have to give up their convenience in order for me to have some convenience. I hated to inconvenience another person. Even if they said, "It was ok," it still bothered me. It was embarrassing and humiliating that so much help was needed. I was a newborn with an advanced degree. My brain wanted to do, but it was not mature enough to do. It was like being inside of that jail cell: the one that surrounded me in flames and captivity.

Thinking about it too much makes you go mad. So for the sake of my wife, my newborn son and all my dreams for my family's life just one short month ago, I decided that I was not going to let this stroke defeat me. It was going to be a fight, a fight with no fear or excuses. Knowing that so much was lost and that it was going to be a hard to get back to life before the stroke, it was what had to be done with no excuses. Too many people were depending on me.

All the dreams of recovery lay ahead of me to walk downtown to get a cup of coffee, play ball with my son as he grew, hold my wife with both arms and stand on my own. It was going to be a fight, a hard fight.

The stroke damaged me physically *and* mentally, and this is true of all stroke victims. The brain thinks with the same pathways we move with. (4) So if movement is impaired, so is thinking. Many stroke survivors have personality changes, depression, intense anger or a desire to withdraw from society. The mental hurdles can prevent the physical from improving. In my case, the mental hurdles cost me the people I loved most.

But back at the rehab hospital, my eyesight and speech were my greatest concern. They were worse than they had been immediately following my stroke as a result of *diaschisis*. I still could not see well enough to distinguish my nurse's face, my therapist's face, or my friends' faces when they visited. Even worse, my son was only two months old and I couldn't see his precious face or that of my wife. This was because the *floculous*, (5) the very specific part of the cerebellum which controls and stabilizes eye movement, had obviously been affected by my stroke.

It was impossible for me to use my arms effectively and the dizziness was intense whenever my head moved. When moving, the room would tip and made me fall. I looked even worse than feeling bad. My face was unshaven, and it felt like my body must have smelled like rotten eggs, although Beth said that it didn't. Thank heaven. It was necessary to ignore this feeling in order to work at all the limitation so that grooming me would be possible again. A hot shower, haircut and a shave was one of my dreams. My first haircut was about three weeks after the stroke. A barber came once a week and had a shop on the bottom floor of the facility. "Just cut it off," I told her.

After the stroke I just wanted it off. She shampooed my hair first. Having her run water over my head felt like weeks of grime was washed away. The soap and the head massage felt luxurious. There was no memory of anyone washing my hair before, so it was the first real treat since the stroke. The mirror was superfluous since it was not possible to see my hair getting cut but the feeling with each clip of the scissor felt lighter. Also as she moved her hands over my head, pulling the hair to cut; my scalp came alive. Rubbing my head with my good hand the short hairs and my clean scalp, my head and body felt for the first time since the stroke clean, light and presentable. But soon the wheel chair is noticed and the reality of my situation came flooding back. Still disabled, still having physical problems, not fully human.

    Losing a considerable amount of weight looking drawn and gaunt, visitors acknowledged the weight loss with a surprised tone at my appearance. The appreciation for the taste of food was lost and, so there was a loss of joy in eating some of my favorite foods. The brain is what allows you to smell, not your nose. With having a brain injury it made sense that my smell was lost. It has been about 16 years since my stroke and it is still difficult for me to smell food, but beginning to get better. Taste is improving although foods have to be well spiced.

There is nothing that does not happen without our brain being involved. Something as simple as a loss of smell can not only be a clue as to what part of the brain is not working but can be an early warning sign of future brain issues, as much as a twenty year warning sign. Little things like not being able to smell and not remembering were the keys are not so much a sign of aging, but possibly the beginning of problems with the brain. So it is important to get that ability to smell back or remember were the keys are. (6)

Several weeks into my rehabilitation, my wife brought me a lemon poppy seed muffin (my favorite) and a cup of coffee. Beth wanted to bring my pre-stroke life back to me to help keep me motivated. I never drank coffee until I met my wife. Beth loves coffee and she converted me into a coffee lover. Now it is hard to know which one of us loves coffee more. At that time any liquids or solid food was forbidden, only thickened liquid. Nevertheless we went outside and Beth snuck the goodies to me. With the first bite, it was a big mistake. It was not possible to swallow so I choked on the muffin. It was pretty desperate and luckily resolved but the incident made my poor wife cry.

This made me realize how bad things were and how much my life will be different. The stroke made me realize how much of life was taken for granted. How precious the little things are when they are no longer possible to do or have.

Subtly and without realizing it my trust in others began to fail. For no reason there was anger, being overly sensitive at the littlest slight, friends and family irritated me. Sorry to say even trusting my wife became difficult. All they wanted to do was help, but it had no effect on my suspicions. Judging them harshly is one of my biggest regrets, it wasn't me, but the effects of the stroke, but that fact doesn't make it any easier to forgive myself. These feelings were kept inside. Hiding from life and others, social situations made me feel very uncomfortable. Imperfection angered me and was harshly judged. Funny how that works, you see the frontal lobe is the part of the brain that makes everything about you *you* and like the *parietal lobe,* (7) it too communicates with the cerebellum. So the stroke slowly changed my personality. It was like developing Alzheimer's.

One of the signs of early Alzheimer's, according to the Alzheimer's association of America is personality changes. (8) In my case it made sense. The stroke affected my left cerebellum, which communicates with my right brain. Most researchers believe that Alzheimer's principally affects the right brain. Also the cerebellum, along with its many functions, coordinates thought. My thoughts were strange due to the five infarcts with one in the *dentate nucleus*, that particular area of the cerebellum which coordinates and affects thought.

There was an exact schedule of activities each day. My therapists helped me stand up and walk. There was a great deal of fear about this. My eyes were constantly moving so it seemed the ground was moving. Unable to fixate on a point to give me a reference trusting my therapists not to let me topple over was important for me to progress. They gave me a lot of encouragement which made it easier to trust them and my legs.

Seeing the world moving and ignoring it made it difficult to trust. It took a while but eventually my eyes settled down and walking and balance became much easier, but walking at night is still difficult. The reason being my eyes help me keep me balanced so in low light it becomes difficult to keep my balance. It took a week or two before I could walk with a walker using their help and even then I walked like a Frankenstein monster.

Initially my therapy consisted of simple activities such as folding towels, putting round pegs into round holes, putting objects like forks and spoons together. My son learned how to walk, talk, and coordinate his movements by living his life. It was like growing up with my son.

Then there was "Thinking Therapy which consisted of someone asking me a series of questions and me answering. It generally consisted of the cognitive therapist reading a story to me, a simple story about a man fixing his car walking his dog or driving to work. In the story there would be descriptions of things the man sees, also dialog with individuals he would meet.

The descriptions would be very colorful and detailed. The conversations were usually simple: "I like your blue shirt," or "your silver car has a rust spot on the left rear fender." After reading the story I would be asked questions about the story. My score would depend on how accurate my answers were. Additional exercises consisted of grouping activities in the right sequence, like get in the car, get gas, and go to the grocery store. Ironically, asked about a sextant I quickly described a sextant as an instrument used to measure the angle between any two visible objects. Yet still my own eyes were having problems measuring distances and angles and details. My answer to the sextant question indicated that my intelligence was not affected by the stroke and gratefully the therapist stopped subjecting me to Thinking Therapy.

All the therapies were fatiguing. This made sense. Research shows that a condition called "Chronic Fatigue Syndrome" (9) is a problem with the brain when it does not get enough of what it needs to function or has suffered some type of injury.

There were many individuals in the same condition. Part of my therapy took place in a room with other brain injury patients, which could be stroke, head trauma, or drug over dose. If the brain is injured it doesn't matter how, the affects can be similar and often are. There, social workers tried to motivate us to share our feelings. The room was always very warm, which made our fatigue only worse. Over and over in my head *I just want to sleep. I just want to sleep.* In fact, many of us did sleep during the sessions.

It was difficult to accept that the time to sleep was not up to me, but the therapist's schedule. Closing my eyes for a few minutes became an overwhelming desire. Close my eyes and sleep after my breakfast, but there were morning therapy sessions. After that, close my eyes and sleep, but there was lunch. After lunch, close my eyes to sleep, but the nurses would not let me lie down after eating because of the fear of aspiration.

Afternoon therapy sessions came next, then dinner and again please let me close my eyes, but that pesky aspiration again. A good night sleep would have made this schedule tolerable, but there was no rest for me later in the evening or during the night because there was an unfortunate fellow down the hall with a severe brain injury which caused him to call for help out loud all night. Poor fellow, but it was interfering with my sleep! Then there was the nurse who would come in my room, turn on the light, check my vitals and give me medication before doing the same for my roommate. Try getting back to sleep after that.

Another major issue was that a brain injury disrupts your nature sleep cycle. (10)Your brain controls everything and my normal circadian rhythm—normal sleep patterns—were disturbed. My sleep hormone (Melatonin) (11) was too low at the beginning of my attempt to sleep and too high in the morning. The reverse goes for the stimulating hormone (Cortisol) (12); it was too high at sleep time and too low in the morning. This normal cycle is controlled by a certain part of the brain called the hippocampus (13). The stroke was in the left cerebellum, which affects the right brain. So it made sense that this was a problem. But it didn't make it any less difficult or frustrating.

    Putting the blankets over my head was an attempt by me to shut out the noise, but the nurse wouldn't let me do that for fear of me suffocating. Next a pillow, but again the nurses discouraged me from using this strategy. Each night desperation creeped in because of the fear of another sleepless night. The lack of sleep got so bad; Beth brought me a radio with headphones. Maybe music could help me sleep. It did help, a nice effect of the type of music (classical) listened to, can stimulate the right brain and the right brain helps you to get to sleep. But even getting to sleep was not enough, the nurse would come in the middle of night to wake me in order to check my blood pressure and to give me pills. It was just not possible to get a good night sleep. It took me months after getting out of the hospital to consistently get a good night sleep.

One night after finally falling asleep, a nurse came in as usual to check my vitals and give me medication. Being groggy from being woken up she gave me pills that seemed to be huge. To this day it is hard to understand why swallowing pills were allowed yet eating solid food was not. Choking on a particularly big pill that night it was lucky that I did not aspirate (have it get into my lungs) the pill although it took several days to get the taste of that pill and the feeling of it out of my throat. It was frustrating to have to worry about such a simple, instinctual thing such as swallowing and this incident made it clear that being careful swallowing was going to be a matter of life or death. To this day there is still trouble swallowing. If I'm careless I will choke on something as simple as a sip of water. One of my vocal cords is still paralyzed. Recently a research article suggested the activity of gargling could help with swallowing and a host of other issues like constipation!

Joe, my roommate, said, "You know what I'm going to do when I get out of here?" I said "What?" "Drag a lawn chair out onto my driveway and watch the world pass. Can you think of anything better?" I couldn't. It was welcome to have a human contact with the same malady even though he was a bit older. Sometimes it seemed God put Joe in that room with me to teach me a lesson. It was a lesson not initially understood, but now it is. Joe was twice my age and had lived a lot of life and was still looking forward to living more no matter what happened to him. There's the lesson. Live life to the fullest, always look for the positive and always dream and have hope, because no matter how bad it is things will change.

Joe had visitors throughout the day and overnight he would yell for help another wake up for me because he couldn't get out of bed on his own. Nevertheless, Joe made a difference in my day. When he was not yelling and was coherent we had some interesting talks. He would reminisce about how he spent his days after retirement. He would sit on a fold-out chair in his driveway with several of his retired buddies having a beer. Talking, looking at the world go by, just enjoying the moment.

To me believe it or not that sounded nice. Imagining Joe sitting there in his driveway made me smile. It was so simple. My dad did that in his retirement. He loved it. It was just beginning to be summer so Joe was looking forward to getting back on that chair with his buddies. He did get discharged before me so I hope he did have a taste of that. He wasn't walking when discharged so I'm not sure if he did. Never hearing nor seeing him again, makes me sad. Another lesson is to make an effort to stay in touch with those that touched your life. Any human contact that involves a shared space and shared malady, requires a certain importance. It is regrettable that I never kept in touch.

    The ward we were in was called the *young stroke ward*, as if being in your eighties is considered young to have a stroke. If so, being 40 must have made me a baby although being there and feeling the way I did my body felt like it was in the eighties. The stroke took years off my life and this was truly a sad time for me. Not sure you would call this depression, which would come later in my recovery, but it was disappointment in myself for having a stroke and being the youngest by decades than other stroke patients. Feeling mortified by being too young in this situation was easy. And in the middle of the night it was easy to go down the dark path. What a horrible position to put my family in. Feeling those thoughts created terrible lonely moments. My Mom used to tell me that it was always darkest before the dawn. But because sleep was so difficult the nights were long and the dawn did not come soon enough during those dark moments. Luckily moving past those thoughts and thinking of the future made it possible for me to move forward. Being a stubborn Polack, I just focused on the task at hand, getting better, not dwelling on my problems and pitying myself. Maybe ignoring these feelings wasn't the best policy, but for the short term it had to. But they would come back to haunt me later.

If there was counseling available at the hospital, I was unaware of it and staff couldn't have been aware of my feelings. The nurses would say how great my motivation was. Their comments were always "you have such a great attitude." My physical therapist would say "Most individuals want to give up but you don't no matter how hard it is." Another said, "No matter what I ask you to do you either do it or at least give it a good try." Another said that "It is good for the other patients to see you try so hard." Looking back it would have been a good idea to at least talk things through with a professional, but that was something that would have to be dealt with later, many years later and many angry uncomfortable moments later.

There was a lot of catching up to do after being away from chiropractic and more specifically chiropractic neurology for seven years. One innovation that developed over that time was a whole field of neuroscience based on the theory of hemispherisity (14). The theory suggests that the sides of the brain have differing functions and likes and dislikes. In other words, what gets the right brain excited is different from what gets the left brain excited. Basically the right brain is the brake pedal and the left brain is the gas pedal. So the right brain is cautious and the left brain gets things done.

So the left brain tends to be critical and exact. It doesn't like change or differences; however the right brain likes differences and tends to be more relaxed about things. In a normal brain this works out fine, but in a brain like mine where the right brain was affected the left brain pushes harder and its' preferences takes over. So being more critical; not liking change or surprises made sense. This was a problem with my wife's family. Normally a relative would just pop over for a visit unannounced. This was unacceptable to my left brain and anger resulted when they did. I, my wife, and her relatives did not understand why anger was my reaction. In light of this theory it became clear.

Another interesting aspect of strokes is an individual's personality or traits that were prevalent before stoke sometimes becomes stronger. I came to learn in my childhood years not to like surprises that were out of my control. When a parent is an alcoholic you are never sure what kind of personality will come through the front door. It could be happy, angry or violent.

Predictability was what made me feel safe. The stroke just made unpredictably more pronounced.

Taking full responsibility for my recovery, chances were taken by me that my traditional therapist thought were risky. They did a wonderful job in helping me recover, but it was important for me to push them to push me. "We have to keep you safe so don't risk falling." My therapist would tell me. But pushing myself was how my symptoms would improve. Walking became very important to me. If my walking got better, other issues would improve. In order for me to get better my eyes had to get better as well. My doctor's said "No matter what you do your eyes will either get better on their own or not at all." That was unacceptable. One therapist stated that "After six months you probably won't get much more improvement." Again that was not for me to believe. In fact I am still getting better and it has been 16 years. After several years of treating stroke survivors myself I can see how difficult it is to keep a patient motivated when progress is very slow. It usually is not a matter of *if*, but a matter of *when*, but many cannot believe they will get well and get discouraged and quit trying. That is painful to see.

Discouragement was not going to get in my way. My recovery was slow and frustrating but believing things were going to get better helped me get better. Visualizing myself walking normally, even reading a book; taking care of myself like shaving, taking a shower, sort of like daydreaming taught my brain that it was possible for me to do those things again. This daydreaming became a matter of habit. It is believed you are what you think. This was another lesson learned. There could no let up on this. Attempting to walk and transfer myself to the wheel chair made my nurses and doctors nervous, since they were worried I'd fall and hurt myself. Being stubborn, their warnings went un-heeded.

My wife, friends and family made it easy for me to focus on my recovery. They did all the back ground stuff, bills, social security, disability, etc. "Just get better," they said.

After about 5 months and a great many false starts, and falls my walking did improve with the use of a walker and with guidance because of my wacky vision. It was glorious to be able to have the confidence to walk and not struggle with every step. The sense of independence just encouraged me to do better to get more independent. Soon walking down town and getting a cup of coffee was going to be a reality. Eventually there was no risk or danger transferring myself from the bed to my wheelchair without assistance. It was liberating not to have to ask someone for help. Life was becoming normal for me. Shaving on my own became possible again, but an electric razor had to be used because of my poor vision. Closing one eye helped my vision but not my dizziness. This strategy helped make it possible for me to move about without falling. Even though this strategy helped, getting my eyes to work together was one of my goals. Showering was not easy since every time I tilted my head, it was like being on a merry-go-round doing cart wheels. It made taking a shower a whole new experience so it was baths for me for a long time.

Beth observed: "I arrived at the rehab facility one night to see Greg in the bathroom getting himself ready for bed. What a relief that was for me, and I am sure for him! Even though he was brushing his teeth while sitting in a wheelchair, which he then wheeled over to his bed and got himself into, it was so encouraging to know he had at least regained that much mobility and ability."

My therapists had me do all kinds of exercises to try to improve my balance and help me walk correctly again. Remembering one afternoon in the rehab room the therapist asked me to climb some stairs, ride a bike, and walk using parallel bars and other activities one right after another. Determined to do anything they asked I did them all without complaint and with glee. It was just important to be moving. The therapist appreciated my commitment and easy going compliant manner since most patients complained and resisted any suggestions. The therapists had to deal with a great deal of negativity. It was and is a thankless job. After my afternoon session there was one patient the therapists were trying to get to stand and walk. The patient kept complaining stating that she couldn't do it. Even though it must have been very difficult for the therapist to deal with her, they treated her with respect and without any judgment. They were great. For my recovery it was important to do the things that were difficult or impossible for me to do, even if I failed. Just like any skill that needs to be learned, there is no substitution in actually performing the skill. To this day this is central to my recovery and how others in my practice are taught to approach their recovery.

Since I was so willing to try anything, my therapist soon had me walking without a walker, but with an Assists Belt —a cloth belt that they wrapped around my waist so that the therapist can support my balance. Using this belt was the closest thing to walking free. Transitioning to the belt was frightening; it felt almost like jumping out of a plane. The belt was the parachute, but you had nothing to hold on to. It was freeing but my vision and balance were awful, which made me put all my trust in the therapist. Since balance depends on the cerebellum and the eyes working in unison it was difficult for me to walk without falling, but the act of walking can and did make the cerebellum work better, even though my eyes didn't. You see the cerebellum helps your balance at night and when your eyes are closed. My trouble was both the eyes and the cerebellum were affected so closing my eyes did not help. But by working on my balance and walking the cerebellum was being strengthened and that was a good thing. This did help to the point where my eyes had less effect on my walking. Walking at night is still troublesome because my cerebellum is still slightly weak from the stroke. Tools called compliant boards or wobble board were used to help exercise my balance. The therapists would have me stand on them and try and keep my balance. Standing on these were like standing on a ship in rough water. By having the give in the board you are forced to compensate to keep yourself upright.

This again exercises the cerebellum. To further challenge my balance, the therapist would have me walk using a rail for security. The first few times were scary, but soon it got easier to do and less frightening. It seemed with my recovery there were lots of leaps of faith.

    I was excited to show Beth the progress I had made with walking. That day the therapist, with the help of an assist belt, walked me around a small atrium surrounded by a railing. It was a long distance for me to walk. She arrived in the afternoon after work. She wheeled me out to the atrium and I proudly pointed to the railing stating "I walked around the entire perimeter today." Unfortunately being too tired from the day's therapy it wasn't possible for me to show her. Several years later Beth explained after that day she was concerned about this small accomplishment. It showed her how much recovery was still ahead for me. As a consequence, Beth felt she couldn't work full time so she declined an opportunity to further her career. She needed to be available to take care of me.

In order to be able to negotiate my home it was necessary to learn how to climb and descend stairs. The therapists had an exercise station comprised of steps just for this purpose. There were only four steps. Up and down hundreds of times, very boring, but challenging.

Desperate to get out of the hospital and home again made me work hard. My days continued to be full of the mundane but necessary therapies of putting round pegs in round holes and square pegs in square holes, folding towels while sitting and standing, rising from a chair to a standing position and sitting down again. All these were designed to attempt to improve my coordination, balance and strength. Therapies also included speech exercises, practice walking with a walker or assist belt, and brain exercises.

For brain exercises, a therapist still thought it was a good idea for me to read and interpret stories. She felt that it would keep my brain healthy. Initially the stories were too simple so she made them more complicated to the point where they couldn't be any more complicated. At least the problem solving and memory part of my brain was okay. One of the lucky consequences of this brain exercise was that it exercised a part of my brain that could have eventually been affected by the stroke. Remember diaschisis? Because my cerebellum was affected, if the parts of my brain which still worked well, weren't kept stimulated they might have eventually been adversely affected. After a brain injury it is necessary to use all parts of your brain, not just the damaged parts. It helps with *neuroplasticity*, which is the brain's ability to reorganize itself by forming new neural connections, and thus helps with the recovery. The damaged parts must be exercised first though and more than the undamaged parts. This will bring the brain into balance.

In my practice many of my patients have this problem, where certain parts of their brain are too strong and overwhelm the other parts. This can result in everything from depression to chronic pain or fatigue. The trick is to identify the weak parts of the brain and design exercises that can make them stronger. This is just one of the things that can be done for brain injury patients, such as those who suffered a stroke. But what is really interesting and powerful is that this type of understanding and therapy can be applied on patients with minor injuries. Studies have shown that minor injuries to an ankle, elbow or any joint can affect the brain. This may be the reason an ankle is easier to re-sprain. The part of the brain that controls the ankle is injured and not coordinating the ankles movement. (15)

    Eating and fatigue remained big problems for me. Eating normal food again, to have a steak, a hamburger, a beer, a candy bar, or just a ham sandwich was still just a dream. One night Beth snuck in her aunt's beef stew. Such a simple thing, but it made me happier than I'd been in a long time. Beth had pureed the stew in a blender in order that it could be swallowed safely. That first taste of mashed up stew was heaven. Beth continued to sneak food in at night, her pureed contraband saved me. While watching me sip my stew Beth asked with a little trace of heartbreak in her voice. "Is it good?" "Better than you'll ever know." Words were not enough to express my gratitude for all the ways she was saving me.

Rotary Nystagmus (16) or involuntary rapid movement of the eyeball was an issue during my entire stay in the rehabilitation hospital. My eyes rotated continually, even when they were closed. There was no way of stopping them. Everything involving my eyes were a challenge. Reading, driving a car watching a tennis match and focusing on a person or thing requires the eyes to be coordinated with each other. My entire world was now rotating and not only that, objects, persons would be duplicated in quadruplets. This was very disorientating and at times rather sickening.

Rotary nystagmus was a big factor contributing to my vertigo and difficulty with walking. Vertigo or balance is coordinated by several parts of the brain and body. (17) If one or more are compromised, it makes it difficult to keep your balance. So the parts of the balance system affected on me were my eyes and the part of the cerebellum that has to do with balance. It was very important to get my eyes under control so that my vision could help my cerebellum work well. The problem was the part of the cerebellum that coordinated the eyes is the same part that helps with balance. This was difficult and made my progress slower. My eyes could not get help from the cerebellum and my cerebellum could not get help from my eyes. My eyes needed to settled down, if there was any chance for me to be able walk correctly again. Unfortunately there were no exercises or therapies anyone knew about then to help me. Luckily my new mantra: "Do what you can't do" eventually solved the problem. What did that mean for my eyes? Simply try to focus them. Sounds crazy, but no one else had an answer, so something had to be tried. My eyes had to learn how to focus again, just like learning how to ride a bike, just do it. Starting with big objects like buildings and gradually focusing on smaller objects. One exercise I discovered was while walking to the gym I would stop and focus on tree bark for 30 seconds, then start walking again. I did this 10 to 12 times a day. Eventually my eyes settled, which helped my cerebellum, which further helped my eyes.

Gradually after long periods of repeatedly doing speech exercises my voice began to improve. Since they were simple, blowing a feather, or saying the vowels over and over again slowly so that my throat would vibrate they did not require support, so they were done on my own. The motivation was if my speech improved, my eating would also. With all this, resting my throat between exercises was very important since there was only one functioning vocal cord. There were no long conversations on the phone. Explaining to my Mother and siblings who lived out of state that I could only say "Hi" was sad. Wanting to talk longer to tell them about my progress was not possible. Even after my speech improved if my throat got tired it could convulse into a coughing frenzy for several minutes. Just a small drop of my own saliva would send me into a coughing spasm.

Swallowing. Something all of us do thousands of times a day without thinking was something that I had to think about. One morning I underwent a video fluoroscopy of my throat while swallowing to determine whether or not I could tolerate regular food. Video fluoroscopy (18) is a video camera with an x-ray machine attached. It was designed in order to see inside the body while it is moving.

This was an unpleasant experience for several reasons. The liquid food was cold and was mixed with barium so that the video camera could see it and show what my throat was doing. The speech therapist could actually see if my swallowing was allowing food into my lungs. Various motions of my neck showed what positions allow the food to go down my esophagus as apposed into my lungs. After several tries in different positions, it was possible for me to swallow without aspirating. It took about an hour of trial and error to get to that point, but at last I was finally cleared to be able to eat normal food again. That very afternoon one of my dreams came true in the form of a hamburger, root beer, and French fries. It was one of the best hamburger, root beer and French fries I ever had. In order to get my taste buds excited they were seasoned with more than the normal amount of pepper and salt. This actually activated my taste buds which drove the neuro connections to my brain, thus teaching my brain to taste again.

    With my therapists' continued aid, my rehab progressed to the point where they trusted me to take an occasional walk unassisted using a walker. Gripping the walker's handles and looking at the ground to try and focus on where my feet were going was exhausting. My brain had to do a lot of work. Even though this was encouraging weeks slipped by and it didn't seem like I was any closer to getting out of the hospital and home. Sleep was still spotty and my weight continued to drop. When my wife brought my son in to visit me, he did nothing but cry. Babies can sense that the hospital wasn't the best place to be and he didn't like it. This crushed me. When my son was born my wish was to be the kind of dad he looked up to and idealized.

Instead, now he cried when he saw me. Feeling like a monster and loser, how was I ever going to get out of this and be the father Alex deserved?

Finally my progress got to the point where it was possible for me to go home for a day visit. My brother John and sister-in-law Susan were visiting from Texas and were there to help me get home and back. They picked me up from the hospital; it was like getting out of prison. As they drove me home the opened window allowed the breeze to kiss my face making me feel alive. Seeing Beth and Alex in our home filled me with both joy and sadness. Somehow by being sick I let them down. Beth was smiling and compassionate, Alex didn't cry when he saw me. That made me feel there was hope that things could get back to normal. Neighbors and friends came to see me. Everyone was caring and happy. To know so many cared was comforting, but also there were feelings of embarrassment that they needed to take care of me so much.

The smell, the sound, the feeling was sweet to me. Home at last, away from the antiseptic hospital with all its smells, sounds and routine. Home again and free if only for a day. Right before the stroke, the second floor of our house had just been remodeled. My neighbors had graciously finished the painting for me. It constantly surprised me all the kindness that was given to me. Realizing how much people cared and wanted to help made me feel truly blessed. Enjoying a home cooked meal, newly painted renovations, siting at the window seat and feeling the breeze from the back yard, was a dream come true. It seemed like my nightmare would be over soon. It was satisfying feeling being home and seeing my son in a different environment than the hospital. Alex not crying was overwhelming. Was it possible he didn't hate me or blame me for not being the dad he wanted? It gave me the impression when he cried that his little brain told him his father got sick so he won't be able to play catch with you or go fishing or long walks with, he cried out of disappointment.   Seeing that he still loved me made my heart sing.

Seeing my family, friends and neighbors motivated me to get better even faster. Longing to stay, but my rehab was not finished.

And I'll be forever grateful for the care the rehab staff gave me for it is not an easy job to take care of stroke victims. We lose all ability to take care of ourselves and become like children again and we can be very stubborn and nasty. The effort and dedication it takes to take care of someone like that is enormous and admirable. Everyone on the staff was cheerful and helpful in difficult situations. They didn't complain to us, but we surely complained to them. Approaching life with grace and ease is not easy, but more is accomplished. My mom always used to tell me "You get more bees with honey than vinegar." She was more correct in that statement than she even realized. Taking people for who they are without judgment and with an open mind and heart can change the world.

In Conclusion

Adversity in life can teach us valuable lessons. We all have people who love us and care about us. If we need help, all we have to do is ask. I hope this 1st book will help someone learn that they are not alone even if they feel they are. How you feel may not be a reality. To find out, take a chance. If you don't try you will never know. Look for the sequels to this book. There is more to learn and understand what it means to be healthy.

References

Prologue

(1) http://www.strokecenter.org/patients/about-stroke/stroke-statistics/

Chapter 1

(1) http://www.chiro.org/LINKS/subluxation.shtml

Chapter 2

(1) http://masscases.com/cases/sjc/358/358mass13.html
(2) https://www.acnb.org/
(3) http://www.ncbi.nlm.nih.gov/pubmed/9345682
(4) http://www.ncbi.nlm.nih.gov/pmc/articles/PMC3760628/

Chapter 3

(1) https://en.wikipedia.org/wiki/Vertebral_artery_dissection
(2) http://medical-dictionary.thefreedictionary.com/nociception
(3) http://medical-dictionary.thefreedictionary.com/diaschisis
(4) http://www.ncbi.nlm.nih.gov/pubmed/17504139

Chapter 4

(1) http://www.ncbi.nlm.nih.gov/pubmed/23816263
(2) http://www.neuromodulationlab.org/index.php?option=com_content&view=article&id=201:brain-stimulation-may-aid-stroke-recovery&catid=162:media-press-releases&Itemid=72
(3) http://www.upmc.com/patients-visitors/education/nutrition/pages/thickened-liquids-nectar-thick.aspx
(4) http://brainconnection.brainhq.com/2013/03/05/the-anatomy-of-movement/
(5) https://en.wikipedia.org/wiki/Flocculus_(cerebellar)

(6) http://blog.odotech.com/part-brain-smell-special-guest-author-edition

(7) http://brainmadesimple.com/parietal-lobe.html

(8) http://www.alz.org/professionals_and_researchers_behavioral_symptoms_pr.asp

(9) http://www.cdc.gov/cfs/

(10) http://science.howstuffworks.com/life/inside-the-mind/human-brain/sleep1.htm

(11) http://dictionary.reference.com/browse/melatonin

(12) http://dictionary.reference.com/browse/cortisol

(13)　http://dictionary.reference.com/browse/hippocampus

(14)　http://www.cuug.ab.ca/dorfsmay/delirium/brain_hemis.html

(15)　http://www.biausa.org/mild-brain-injury.htm

(16)　https://en.wikipedia.org/wiki/Nystagmus

(17)　https://en.wikipedia.org/wiki/Balance_disorder

(18)　http://www.encyclopedia.com/doc/1O62-videofluoroscopy.html

Made in the USA
Middletown, DE
16 September 2020